CLIMATE HERO HANDBOOK

How Kids Can Defend, Protect, and Restore the Planet

Jennifer Manley Rogers
and Jessica Gamaché

Illustrated by Sophie Anne Elliott

HIGHER EDUCATION & MINISTRY
General Board of Higher Education and Ministry
THE UNITED METHODIST CHURCH

To my parents, for the gift of my own in-the-wild childhood.
And to my three greatest gifts, my children.—JMR

To the climate heroes who encouraged me
on this journey.—JG

HIGHER EDUCATION & MINISTRY
General Board of Higher Education and Ministry
THE UNITED METHODIST CHURCH

By taking a long and thoughtful look at what
God has made, people have always been able
to see eternal power . . . and the mystery
of God's being.

—Romans 1:20 (MSG)

All we have to do is wake up
and change.

—Greta Thunberg

Contents

WATER

ANIMALS

An Invitation

The pages of this book include pictures and stories about sleeping trees, ocean-crossing whales, and many other wondrous things found on the earth. These pages also share how Climate Heroes can appreciate and care for this incredible planet we call home.

Climate Heroes take action when they see the negative impact that humans have on the warming and cooling of the earth. They value and protect the land, air, water, and animals that make up our world. These four things are seen and written about often in this book, as a reminder. Without them, life could not be.

The moment you picked up this book your Climate Hero training began. All that's required now is an open mind to keep reading, a pencil to draw or write down your thoughts and make plans, and the will to act.

Be curious and learn all you can about the natural world around you, with this book as your guide. The more time a Climate Hero spends exploring and experiencing nature, the more they'll defend the earth. Even small changes can ripple out and make a big difference.

As you read, look for pictures of a young person like you, dressed in a hoodie and armed with this book, exploring, learning, and acting on behalf of a healthier planet. This is a Climate Hero in the making. Toward the end of the book you'll see this figure transform into a Climate Superhero, decked out in cape and armor. Don't be surprised if you transform, too.

. . . to Be a Climate Hero

Those who contemplate
the beauty of the earth find reserves
of strength that endure.
—Rachel Carson,
writer, scientist, ecologist

LAND

Nature Observation Station

Pick a place where you can go to observe nature and enjoy the beauty and wonder it so generously gives. Climb a tree, sit on a park bench, lean against a rock, crouch next to a creek—these are just a few possibilities. Let your sense of wonder lead you.

Before you visit your station, remember to dress for the weather. Carry this book and a pencil with you, so you can take notes and draw what you see. If you are with a friend, make a pact to remain quiet while you watch your surroundings. Be still and aware of the living things that are near. Look for tracks, trails, holes, nests, feathers, fur, insects, and animals. Then listen. Do you hear wind? birds? foraging animals? running water? Be sure to record your experience on pages 8 and 9. Don't forget to look above and beneath you! Life is everywhere.

Once you return home, read over your notes and learn more about what you saw by asking questions and investigating further. Most of all, express gratitude on your journal page for all the living things that make this a beautiful, balanced, healthy, and healing world.

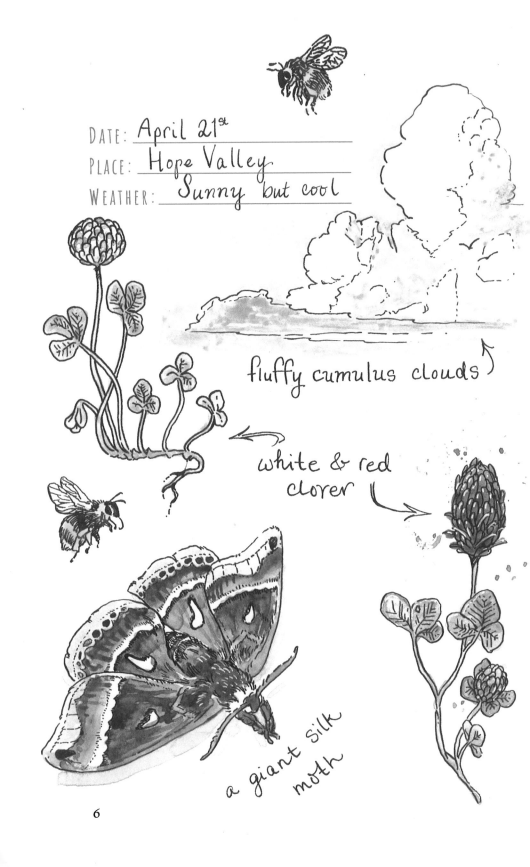

DATE: April 21st
PLACE: Hope Valley
WEATHER: Sunny but cool

fluffy cumulus clouds

white & red clover

a giant silk moth

Sample Nature Journal Page

flowering
blackberries

dancing barn swallows

I found a hawk feather!

puzzlegrass
growing everywhere

7

MY NATURE JOURNAL PAGE

DATE: _____

PLACE: _____

WEATHER: _____

9

Trees, the Planet's Superpower

Has a tree ever caught your attention, perhaps a young sapling growing through a crack in the sidewalk or an older tree that seems to have a friendly face in the shape of its bark? If you don't have a favorite tree *yet*, take this moment to make one your very own. It can be a living tree or one you have seen in a book or on the internet. Write about such a tree on the next page.

Describe your tree and its location, size, and shape. Why are you drawn to it?

_____

_____

_____

_____

_____

What type of tree is it? Does it flower during one season and shed its leaves in another? Is it an evergreen tree (one that is green year round)?

_____

_____

ginkgo leaves

Have you ever climbed a tree or picked up blossoms, needles, leaves, nuts, acorns, or pinecones from the ground? If not, hunt for these things. Look closely at what you find and write about it.

_____

_____

_____

If you can, lie under a tree and look up at the sky through its branches. Watch for birds landing on its limbs and insects crawling up its trunk. Take a deep breath and appreciate what trees give us. Express your gratitude in the space below.

_____

_____

_____

Forest Cities and Super Trees

In addition to being majestic providers of food and shade, trees are awesome Climate Heroes and great at fighting pollution. Trees trap and store away carbon dioxide that comes out of smokestacks and tailpipes. This is helpful, as too many carbon emissions cause the earth's atmosphere to overheat, harming the delicate balance of the living world.

Because green leafy things are powerful at cleaning the air and providing oxygen to breathe, planners have begun to build *forest cities and towers*, where the sides of buildings, balconies, roofs, and grounds are covered with thousands of trees and plants. Such plants reduce noise, attract wildlife, and keep the city from becoming too hot during warm seasons. Research also shows that a higher number of trees in a city helps people worry less and gives them a sense of happiness and peace.

Do you think you would like to live in a forest city? How else might cities of the future be designed in order to protect the earth and improve our way of living? No matter where you live or how old you are, as a Climate Hero you can plant trees. Here are some ideas:

- ≪ Plant a young tree in a container and set it on a sidewalk, fire escape, or stoop.

- ≪ Ask for a tree for your birthday and, with family and friends, plant it in your community.

- ≪ Collect money from neighbors to buy a tree and plant it together in your neighborhood.

- ≪ Make arrangements for a tree to be planted in a national or state forest in honor or memory of someone you love.

Although the use of fossil fuels needs to end so that the planet can maintain safe temperatures, planting more trees and restoring forests are excellent ways for Climate Heroes to protect the earth.

Trees and Zzzzzs

After working all day to clean the air and provide us with shade, food, and oxygen, trees deserve a good night's sleep. When the sun sets, tree limbs droop down four inches—a form of sleeping. Like all living things, trees need regular periods of rest.

Trees are remarkable and without them we couldn't survive. They do more than their share to provide, protect, and preserve life at its best on our planet. As Climate Heroes we can join their efforts by planting more trees to help care for the world in which we live.

Live in the sunshine,
swim the sea,
drink the wild air.
—Ralph Waldo Emerson,
author, philosopher, poet

AIR

Forest fires are one source of air pollution. Firefighting pilots provide much-needed support to crews on the ground. They dump water to create a safety zone for firefighters.

Air All Around Us

Even though we can't see it, clean air is one of the most important things in life. The air we breathe not only keeps us alive but determines how good our life and health will be. Air is always moving around us and holds the oxygen that people and animals need to live. If our air is polluted, it means that harmful particles and gases are suspended within it and can enter our bodies. Some particles come from natural sources like wildfires and volcanoes, but more often they are created by exhaust from vehicles and factories.

What Is Ozone?

The earth has an important layer of gases that protects us from most of the harmful parts of the sun's rays that can give us a sunburn. This invisible layer of gases is called the *ozone*, found 10 to 25 miles (15–40 kilometers) above our heads. Sometimes these same ozone gases, created by cars and factories, linger at ground level, too, where we walk and play. Children, the elderly, and people with health concerns are most at risk from ground-level ozone.

Greenhouse Gases

Greenhouse gases are those that trap energy from the sun and cause the temperature on earth to rise. Pollution from cars and factories causes these gases to increase in our atmosphere, and this has a long-term global health impact. Excess heating causes the melting of ice caps and extreme weather. Warmer weather also makes it harder for farmers to grow crops. All of these factors are due to an increase in greenhouse gasses.

Heroic Choices

Now that you know about air pollution and greenhouse gases, you and the people you know can do the things in the list below each day to fight air pollution as Climate Heroes! Check each one off as you go. Remember, any choice you make that reduces the use of energy makes you a Climate Hero and keeps our atmosphere and planet clean.

- Choose public transportation such as buses or trains.
- Organize and combine errands into one trip.
- Start a recycling program in your neighborhood or school.
- Remove any unnecessary items that weigh down your car.
- Turn off the lights when you leave a room.
- Use energy-saving lightbulbs.
- As often as possible, open windows and use a fan instead of air conditioning.
- Set your thermostat to 78° F in hot months and 68° F in cold ones.
- Wash laundry in cold water and line dry.
- Use a microwave or toaster instead of an oven for small meals.
- Carry reusable shopping bags in your purse or car and avoid plastic bags.
- Enjoy "green" outdoor activities, including camping, biking, and hiking.
- Grow plants that don't require much water.
- Bring your lunch or walk to a nearby restaurant to reduce auto emissions.

Learning about ozone, greenhouse gases, and making heroic choices takes brain power. But it's wise to give your mind a break from time to time, as part of staying strong and healthy. Have a friend or family member read this page aloud to you and follow their instructions. Enjoy this time tuning in to yourself and nature.

Peaceful Observation

1 As you move through your day, notice the wind as it shifts tree branches, blows leaves on your path, or touches your face.

2 If you are able, step outside and find a place to sit. Then, look for signs of wind. If you aren't able to go outside, look out your door or window. Or, imagine you are watching the wind blow gently.

3 What do you see? Focus on just one thing that is stirring in the breeze. It may be a slow-moving cloud, a leaf dangling from a limb, a flag whipping in the wind, or a plastic bag blowing down the street.

4 Watch the object you've decided to focus on and now notice your breathing. Breathe in and out, deeply at first, and then with ease.

5 Now count your breaths. If a new thought happens to enter your mind, gently bring your focus back to your counting and breathing.

6 As you breathe in, imagine air entering your lungs, filling you with peace. When you breathe out, feel grateful for life-giving air.

7 Keep breathing deeply for a few more minutes. You may even close your eyes for a while. Open your eyes when you feel ready.

Circle the words below that describe what you felt during your time in peaceful observation. What other words or thoughts express the sensation of watching the wind blow and feeling air enter your lungs?

Quiet Peaceful Aware Restless
Sleepy Grateful Calm

_____

_____

_____

Remember, you can practice peaceful observation at any time. It's a good way to tune in to your self, your body, and the world around you. This regular practice will bring you feelings of rest and calm. Draw and write on the journal pages that follow to record your reflections.

The earliest record of a wind-powered ship under sail appears as an image on a 6,000-year-old Egyptian vase.

My Peaceful Observation Page

flower chafer beetle

DATE: _____

PLACE: _____

WEATHER: _____

Can you find the following things that show the presence of wind and air moving in our world? Make a check mark next to the items that you see.

- ❑ Wind turbines spinning
- ❑ Pinwheel spinning
- ❑ Clouds floating
- ❑ Birds flying
- ❑ Kite flying
- ❑ Clothes drying on a laundry line
- ❑ Flags flying
- ❑ Wind chimes ringing

Move Like a Hero

The movement of people and things, called transportation, is necessary for all. But the fuels that we use to run cars, trucks, ships, and planes are major polluters of the air. Moving food from farms to stores, so people can buy it easily, also contributes to air pollution. So, as much as possible, buy food that has been grown or produced close to your home.

Not all types of transportation are equal. Choosing the type that is better for the planet, depending on the need and situation, is a key trait of every Climate Hero. From the list below, pick the heroic choice and check your answers on the bottom of page 29.

Circle the Best Option, Whether A or B:

A   Driving to the grocery store once a week instead of 3 separate times.

B   Carpooling to the grocery store with a friend once a week.

A   25 students riding to a field trip in 8 cars.

B   25 students riding to a field trip on a bus.

A   Riding the bus five blocks from the school to the soccer field.

B   Riding your bike five blocks from the school to the soccer field.

A   Taking a long trip with your family by plane.

B   Taking a long trip with your family by train.

If you're able to be outdoors and breathe fresh air today, be sure
to appreciate that sensation of wind moving around you! Share with
others how, as a Climate Hero, you've made choices such as the ones
listed in this book, and encourage them to make earth-friendly choices
alongside you.

(B is the correct answer to all items on page 28.)

Even if you never have the chance
to see or touch the ocean, the ocean
touches you with every breath you take,
every drop of water you drink,
every bite you consume.

—Sylvia Alice Earle,
marine biologist, oceanographer, explorer

WATER

Oceans and Ourselves

Oxygen, an important part of the air we breathe, is produced by plants that grow in the ocean, primarily vast amounts of a microscopic marine algae called *phytoplankton*. Nearly everything in the world depends on this tiny life-giving plant in some way, even though we can't see it with just our eyes unless it's viewed in a large group. For example, the humpback whale, one of the largest creatures on earth, eats five thousand pounds of plankton a day to survive. In turn, whales contribute to the oxygen we breathe by providing key nutrients through their waste

that nourish phytoplankton, keeping it healthy and alive. What an unlikely partnership—in a balanced ecosystem, whales and phytoplankton are just one life-giving cycle below the surface of our seas, and we couldn't go about our lives on land without them.

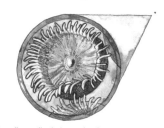

One "piece" of phytoplankton is 20 microns in size. A grain of sand is 90 microns.

Climate Heroes can keep the oceans clean for the sake of these mighty plants and animals by not using single-use plastic items, such as water bottles, wrappers, and grocery bags. Disposable plastic often ends up in the sea and harms marine life because when plastics break down over time they release harmful chemicals. Sadly, a whale was found washed up on shore once with more than 48 pounds of plastic inside it. Even on land, recycling options for single-use plastics are limited and costly. When it comes to this type of plastic, everyone and everything loses.

One important way to fight pollution is to ban single-use plastic. You can lead the way:

- ◌ Boycott single-use plastic and participate in plastic-bag bans.
- ◌ Sign petitions online asking corporations to ban single-use plastic.
- ◌ Talk to restaurants and others about making better choices instead of serving products in disposable plastic, and reach out to companies with this message.
- ◌ Tell your government representatives you want single-use plastic out of your community, if your city or state doesn't have a ban already.

My Inventory of Single-Use Plastic

1 On the following page, note the days you use plastic and what type.

2 Make a mark for each plastic item in its row, then add up your score at the end of the week.

3 Try to reduce your score in the coming weeks.

Keeping this inventory will make you aware of your impact on the earth and help you break the disposable-plastic habit. You can encourage your friends to avoid these plastics as well. Be kind to yourself and each other as you grow and learn these new habits. Soon you'll be single-use plastic free!

Before you start, collect and organize reusable containers and bags in a designated space in your kitchen and use them instead of disposable options. This will help you break the one-and-done plastic habit.

By using less plastic, you protect living things in our oceans, including humpback whales, puffer fish, seaweed, sea fans, sea turtles, and eels. Turn the page and try to find these in the illustration.

PLASTIC					
	bottles	shopping bags	food storage bags	utensils	other
Example	I	I	III	II	I
Day 1					
Day 2					
Day 3					
Day 4					
Day 5					
Day 6					
Day 7					
TOTAL					

The Gift of Water

Water makes it possible for all living things on the planet to live. Except for life found in the sea, plants and animals need *fresh water* to stay alive. In some places, water is so rare that girls and women spend hours each day seeking out and carrying heavy loads of it back to their homes. If we don't protect our fresh water, in time it will run out.

Young girls in Asia and other parts of the world are expected to fetch clean drinking water for their families. Many aren't able to attend school because they have to walk so far for this chore.

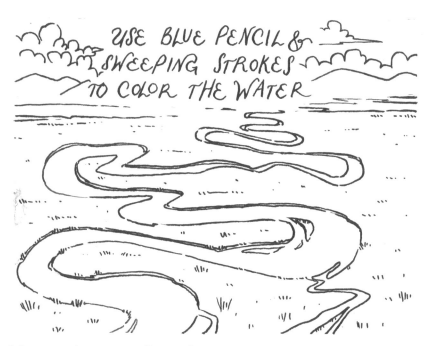

Inlets, seen above, are small arms of a sea, lake, or river. Inlets are key parts of a watershed and the water cycle.

Fresh water falls as rain, moves across the earth in rivers, and enters lakes and seas. This pattern is part of the *water cycle*, and thanks to it, fresh water fills our glasses so we can drink, waters our gardens so we can eat, and washes our clothes and bodies so we can be healthy. Our job as Climate Heroes, in return, is to keep the earth's fresh water clean.

But when we aren't careful, chemicals and waste from farms, factories, and homes pollute fresh water. We can stop everyday toxins from entering our water supply, keeping it safe to drink and protecting our planet.

Only 3 percent of all water on earth is fresh water. Most fresh water is held in unreachable places such as the polar ice caps. This means all life on earth is sustained by less than 1 percent of the planet's water.

Make a Model Watershed

Watersheds are an important part of the water cycle. Imagine rain falling on a mountain top. Those rain drops either soak into the ground or roll into a stream, becoming part of a river, lake, or ocean. The path rainwater takes after it falls to the earth depends on the shape of the watershed.

One way to understand a watershed is to:

1 Tear out page 41 of this book and crumple it into a ball.

2 Smooth out the page slightly with your hands. Be sure to leave some bumps so that the page isn't too flat. This page is now a model watershed. The bumps are hills and mountains. The dips are valleys and rivers.

3 Spray or sprinkle water onto the paper (or just imagine you are doing so)—this is rain falling on your watershed.

4 Observe what happens to the water. Does it soak into the paper? Does it run down the ridges and hills into the valleys and rivers, then drain off the page?

In a real watershed, rain soaks into the ground or travels in streams all the way to a larger body of water. But the moving water can carry pollutants and toxins with it to areas where people and animals live and drink. That is why it is important to protect our watersheds.

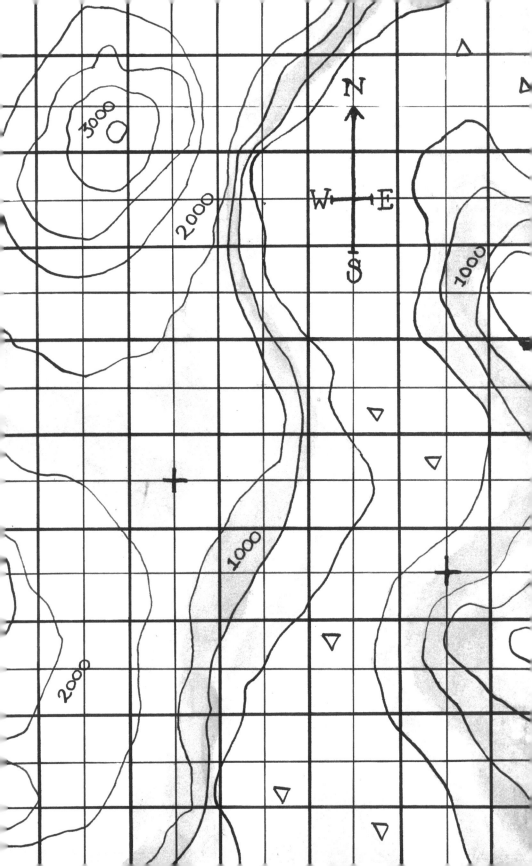

tear out this page

Take Action

The following list shares ways to protect fresh water sources and prevent pollution from entering watersheds.

Put a check by the things you are doing already.
Circle the things you can do.

- Take shorter showers.
- Fix leaky faucets and toilets.
- Turn off the water while brushing your teeth.
- Eat more fruits and vegetables, which require less water to produce than meat.
- Pick up after your dog and dispose of it in the trash.
- Don't pour grease or chemicals down drains.
- Use hardy plants in your yard that don't require fertilizer or lots of water to live.
- Drink tap water instead of bottled water.
- Pick up trash from ditches and roads.
- Sweep instead of hosing off driveways and sidewalks.

What else can you do to conserve and protect our water?

_____   _____

_____   _____

_____   _____

As you walk, look around . . .
reflect . . . dream. Every moment of
the present contains the seeds of
opportunity for change. Your life is
an adventure. Live it fully.

—John Francis,
author, teacher, planet walker

ANIMALS

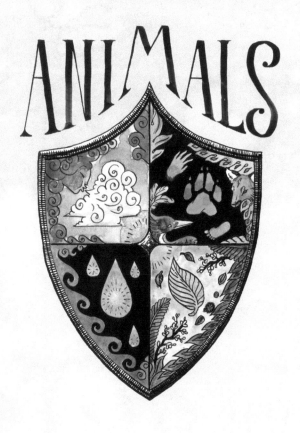

Can you spot a change in the Climate Hero?

Saving Endangered Species

An animal is known as endangered when there are so few left alive that they could disappear from the planet forever. We call animals in such danger *threatened* or *endangered species,* because they are at risk of extinction.

Species: A kind of living thing. For example, a cat, a bear, or a human.

Thankfully, many animals that were once in danger are increasing in number, as Climate Heroes have worked to protect these animals and their natural habitats. But there is much work left to be done—over 1,500 species in the world are currently endangered.

Extinction: The dying out or disappearance of a species from earth.

Climate Heroes never harm living things, including animals and the habitats in which they live. Every animal species is unique, has value, and plays a special role on the earth. It's important to learn about the endangered species in your area and act on their behalf.

- Drive slowly and watch out for wildlife.
- Don't disturb animal habitat, such as logs or piles of leaves and stones.
- Pick up trash and don't pollute.
- Sketch or take a picture of an animal in the wild instead of removing it from its home.
- Speak out on behalf of animals that are threatened.

Success Story

The peregrine falcon is a strong and fast-flying bird of prey that reaches 200 miles per hour when it dives while hunting. These falcons live all over the world, but they were almost completely wiped out by poisons used to protect farmland from insects and other pests in the 1950s.

Because Climate Heroes wrote books and letters about the dangers of pesticides, laws changed, and the peregrine falcon survived instead of dying out forever. This majestic bird of prey can now be seen living in large numbers in both cities and coastal areas.

Still in Danger

The red wolf is one of the most threatened species in North America. Less than 35 red wolves live wild in the United States. Red wolves are called a *keystone species*, because when they live in an area other animals living in the same area have a better, more balanced life.

DRAWING ANIMALS

RED
WOLF

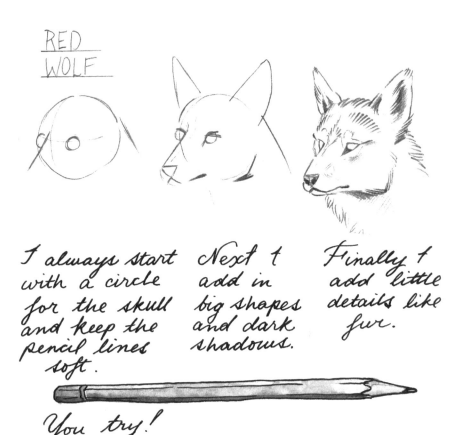

I always start
with a circle
for the skull
and keep the
pencil lines
soft.

Next I
add in
big shapes
and dark
shadows.

Finally I
add little
details like
fur.

You try!

I practice a lot and use a photo reference.

PEREGRINE
FALCON

I press gently with the pencil and draw all big shapes.

Look at the body of the animal and its silhouette.

Save markings and details until the end.

Draw an animal:

Speak Out

Climate Heroes can help save red wolves and other endangered species by remembering to reduce, reuse, and recycle—in that order. The less we use the earth's resources, the less pressure we put on the animals who share the earth and are trying to survive. It's also important to speak out about endangered species. Tell friends, family, and classmates they need our help, then join together to sign petitions and write letters to lawmakers, so that these animals have the land and safety they need.

Friends of the Earth

Many animals are found in this book, from woodpeckers to humpback whales, and each plays its part to maintain a healthy and balanced planet. Woodpeckers keep high levels of insects and pests from killing trees, while trees help fight air pollution and provide oxygen, food, and shelter. This is just one example of a life-giving friendship in nature.

People are animals, too, and we're *interconnected* with all living things, plants and animals alike. How we relate to nature truly matters! And everyone living on our planet has an important calling, to defend, protect, and restore the planet in ways that no other species can. Each day Climate Heroes ask themselves,

Tengmalm's Owl

"Do the choices I make show I'm a friend of the earth?"

As we live on the earth's surface, we have an impact on its cycles, rhythms, and health. Like other animals, we eat, sleep, think, and interact daily. Yet one thing we do, on a higher level, is talk to each other, share information, and teach each other. These skills are key to caring for our environment. We can do more good things for the earth when we join together.

It's important to talk to each other about our love and respect for the earth, share how we care for it, and teach others to do the same. A great way to start is to let our lives and habits be an example as we put the Climate Hero tips in this book into practice. Heroes create *an even better world* for all natural and living things not just today but in days to come.

The Power of the Pen

You can use your creative mind and talent to show appreciation for all the earth gives us.

1 Look through this book and pick out the words that mean the most to you when you think of caring for the planet.

2 Create a word collage, like the one shown below, in the space provided.

3 Write the words you choose in different styles, either in cursive or print. Try using fancy and plain lettering.

4 Share your collage with others to inspire them, and feel free to illustrate your collage by drawing pictures, too.

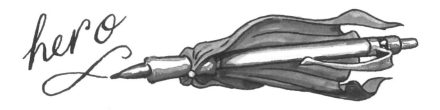

Your pen or pencil takes on a new power when you use it to write your name on petitions for the sake of the earth. A *petition* is a written request that is signed by many people. It asks those who run our government and create laws to make changes for the better. There are petitions online that we can sign to protect land, air, water, and animals.

With a trusted adult, search the internet and start signing petitions for those things that you want to defend! Climate Heroes are protectors willing to make their voices heard.

Science in Action

Did you know that ordinary people, including kids like you, can look at the world around them and send in the information they collect, called *data*, to scientists? Scientists then use this data to help them better track and understand nature. This is called citizen science, and it's another exciting way kids can be Climate Heroes.

Here are a few things that are common to all citizen science projects:

1 Anyone can participate.

2 Participants follow the same guidelines, so high-quality data can be combined and made useful.

3 The data collected is meaningful to real scientists.

4 Without the help of citizen scientists, key data would be missing.

Citizen science projects are easy to find on the internet. For example, one needs citizens to photograph birds with bugs in their beaks, in order to understand bird diet and the balance of nature. Another project asks kids to take pictures of a nearby stream or creek. Sharing this data helps to map water sources across the country and keep them healthy.

With a teacher or other trusted adult, search "kids' citizen science projects" online. One helpful website is SciStarter (https://scistarter.org/).

Many young people who are involved with citizen science projects grow up to be teachers, scientists, biologists, journalists, nature photographers, and other types of Climate Heroes. What job might you have some day?

Attention Activists!

One way a Climate Hero can teach others to love and care for the planet is to be an activist for the earth. What is an activist?

An activist is a person who works to make a positive change or stop something harmful.

An *environmental* activist is a person who is aware of all living things and chooses to be their protector. Being such an activist means looking out for fragile living things and preserving natural beauty. Some of the bravest activists are young people just like you. You can read more about their lives in the Climate Hero Hall of Fame on pages 60–63.

Whether through artwork, signing petitions, citizen science projects, or activism, there are countless ways to show your appreciation for the planet as you defend, protect, and restore it. In this way, Climate Heroes lead others in their efforts to care for the planet.

Write down ways you will be a Climate Hero in the coming week, and stay strong on your path as a friend of the earth *every* week!

_____

_____

_____

_____

_____

_____

_____

_____

_____

_____

_____

CLIMATE HERO
HALL OF FAME

Lesein Mutunkei
Nairobi, Kenya

Lesein Mutunkei is now a teenager, but he started planting trees to counter climate change as a young boy. He says to all kids, "It does not matter how small you are, everything you do for the environment counts. I am fifteen years old now and I love football and outdoor adventure. I understood the impact of cutting down trees, climate change, and plastic pollution when I was about 11 years old."

Because of Lesein's concern for the planet, he decided to do something even bigger as a Climate Hero: he combined his love for football and nature. He decided that for every goal he scored in a game, he would plant a tree. The idea stuck, and with his leadership he started Trees for Goals.

Every time a goal was scored by his team, eleven trees were planted. The number eleven was chosen because it's the number of teammates on a football team. Eleven is a symbol of the teamwork needed to take on climate change and be a part of solutions.

Then Lesein's school rugby *and* basketball teams borrowed his Trees for Goals idea. When goals were scored in any game, trees were planted. Soon nearly 1,000 new trees were put into the ground, to fight back against deforestation.

Lesein's work as a Climate Hero led him to speak at the United Nations Youth Climate Summit about better care for the planet. And knowing that he is doing something good for the earth when he scores a goal makes Lesein play football all the better.

Licypriya Kangujam
Manipur, India

Licypriya Kangujam lives in India. Many schools in her country have been ordered to close because air pollution has become too thick and reached unhealthy levels. She has asked for new laws that will help ensure cleaner air.

Although Licypriya is one of the youngest to do so, with great courage she spoke in front of world leaders at the United Nations Climate Change Conference. She asked leaders to make a cleaner world. Licypriya says she felt led to speak out and ask for government action to solve pollution problems after seeing others do the same.

Licypriya also wants lessons on climate change and caring for the planet to be taught in all schools. Because she has spoken out for this, two states in her country now have programs in schools that teach about climate change.

As more kids learn about caring for the planet, just as you learn by reading this handbook, the world will be full of Climate Heroes. Together, we can make the world a cleaner place to live and breathe.

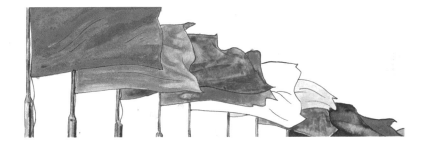

Mari Copeny
Flint, Michigan, USA

When Mari Copeny was eight years old, she wrote to the president of the United States, Barack Obama. She wanted him to know what was going on in her hometown of Flint, Michigan. A dirty river full of toxins was the source of her town's water. This water was making people sick, especially kids like her. It wasn't safe to drink from the faucets at home or to bathe or shower, because the poisoned water caused skin rashes. Any time Mari's family needed to brush their teeth, cook, or bathe, they had to use bottled water brought in from a safe source.

Because Mari spoke out, many others gave money and worked to improve the water problem. Together they had hope and were able to hang on until better water was a daily part of their lives again. As Mari says, "Kids need to see themselves as superheroes." From her first day as an advocate until now, Mari has continued to be a Climate Hero.

Since writing her letter to President Obama, Mari has met two other presidents. She is also a proud national youth ambassador for the Climate March. No matter how old you are, where you live, or what the problem, be like Mari—speak out and work for change. Be a Climate Hero!

Sophia Hou

Short Hills, New Jersey,
USA

TIME for Kids is an online magazine made up of writing by young reporters. One of the reporters is Sophia Hou, an eleven-year-old who cares deeply for at-risk and endangered animals. Sophia is a Climate Hero who uses her writing skills to share her passion.

Sophia first wrote a *TIME for Kids* article about a nursery for at-risk kittens and older cats in an animal hospital. This nursery gives special treatment to unhealthy cats so they can heal and grow stronger. Sophie also cares about sea turtles, and she wrote another *TIME for Kids* article about them. As Sophia shares, "Sea turtles live all over the world. They live near coasts and in open waters. All of them are at risk."

One key skill that Sophia has as a reporter is interviewing experts. When she writes, she includes facts shared by scientists and others who work to protect animals.

Through her writing, Sophia is able to educate others about the things that threaten animals. For example, sea turtles love to eat jelly fish. Sometimes sea turtles mistake trash, such as plastic bags floating in the ocean, for a snack. But when sea turtles eat plastic it harms them. In Sophia's writing, she shares solutions to this problem, such as picking up trash on the beach and recycling it properly. Through her hard work as a writer and reporter, Sophia has found a way that is unique to her to be a Climate Hero. Through her reporting, she helps others to learn and be heroic as well.

SCAVENGER HUNT

A scavenger hunt is a game in which someone looks for a number of things that are hidden. Usually the hunt is for something outdoors, but you can play within the very pages of your *Climate Hero Handbook*, to sharpen your eyes for future nature watching!

For this scavenger hunt, look for woodpeckers. Many cultures consider the woodpecker to be a beautiful bird that is hard working, strong, and determined. They are also some of the smartest birds in the world. Woodpeckers are fellow Climate Heroes who keep trees healthy by eating insects when there are too many in an area.

Start from the beginning of this book and, as you turn the pages, look at each illustration. How many woodpeckers can you find in the entire book? Can you spot the woodpecker button on the Climate Hero's backpack? See the illustrations below for a few more clues! Answers are found at the bottom of this page.

Now that you have practiced searching for woodpeckers in this book, take your search outside! Observe and learn about the birds and other animals in your area, to enrich your life and protect them.

(13 woodpeckers can be found in this book. See pages 5, 9, 10, 26, 53, 59, and 64. There is also a woodpecker on every shield.)

CERTIFICATE OF ACHIEVEMENT

Proudly Presented

to Climate Hero

_____

(YOUR NAME)

For Reading and Completing
the *Climate Hero Handbook*

*"Helping to
Defend, Protect,
and Restore
the Planet"*

Glossary

activist: a person who believes in taking action for positive results

advocate: one who supports or promotes the interests of a cause or group

atmosphere: the air in a particular place; the whole mass of air surrounding the earth

balance: harmony; steadiness

boycott: to join with others in refusing to interact with a person, company, or organization in order to communicate disapproval or concern

carbon dioxide: released into the atmosphere when fossil fuels (coal, natural gas, and oil) are burned

community: the people living in an area

corporation: a group that carries on an activity or business

disposable: made to be thrown away after use

ecosystem: an ecological community of living things interacting with their environment, especially in nature

evergreen: having leaves that remain green and functional through more than one growing season

forest: a dense growth of trees and underbrush covering a large area

fossil fuels: made from decomposing plants and animals; when burned, they release planet-warming greenhouse gas emissions

gratitude: the state of being thankful and grateful

inventory: a complete list of items

investigation: a close study or examination

magnification: the apparent enlargement of an object

marine: of or related to the sea

microscopic: very small; only seen with a microscope

nutrient: a substance that provides nourishment

observation: an act or the power of seeing or fixing the mind upon something

organize: to put in order

oxygen: a reactive element that is found in water, in rocks, and free as a colorless, tasteless, odorless gas that forms about 21 percent of the atmosphere; that is capable of combining with almost all elements; and that is necessary for life

petition: a written request made to an authority

pollution: a substance or thing that has harmful or poisonous effects

preserve: to keep or save from injury, loss, or ruin

recycling: processing older materials in order to reuse them

representative: a person who represents a community in a legislative body, especially a member of the US House of Representatives or a lower house in certain state legislatures

restoration: the action of returning something to a former, usually better, condition

sapling: a young tree

single-use plastic: plastic container or item that is designed and sold to be used only once or a few times and then discarded

sustain: to give support or relief to

toxin: poison

wildlife: nonhuman living things, especially wild animals living in their natural environment

Sources

Aldred, Jessica. "The Surprising Role of Whales in Ocean Carbon Capture," *Maritime Executive*, April 24, 2020. https://www.maritime-executive.com/editorials/the-surprising-role-of-whales-in-ocean-carbon-capture.

American Academy of Pediatrics. "Climate Change and Children's Health," 2015. https://www.aap.org/en-us/advocacy-and-policy/aap-health-initiatives/climate-change/Pages/Climate-Change-and-Childrens-Health.aspx.

American Psychological Association. "Mental Health and Our Changing Climate: Impacts, Implications, and Guidance," March 2017. https://www.apa.org/news/press/releases/2017/03/mental-health-climate.pdf.

BBC. "India Climate Activist Licypriya Kangujam on Why She Took a Stand," Feb. 6, 2020. https://www.bbc.com/news/world-asia-india-51399721.

Burke, Susie E. L., Anne V. Sanson, and Judith Van Hoorn. "The Psychological Effects of Climate Change on Children," *Current Psychiatry Reports* 20: 35 (2018).

Butler, Andrew, and Ingrid Sarlov-Herlin. "Changing Landscape Identity: Practice, Plurality, and Power," *Landscape Research Journal* 44, no. 3 (March 2, 2019).

Carson, Rachel. *The Sense of Wonder: A Celebration of Nature for Parents and Children.* New York: Harper, 1956.

Detroit News. "Flint Safe Water Advocate Mari Copeny Is Billboard Awards' Change-maker," May 16, 2022. https://www.detroitnews.com/story/news/local/michigan/2022/05/16/flint-safe-water-advocate-mari-copeny-billboard-awards-changemaker/9789850002/.

Heller, Martin. "Food Product Environmental Footprint Literature Summary: Food Transportation," Center for Sustainable Systems, University of Michigan, Sept. 2017. https://www.oregon.gov/deq/FilterDocs/PEF-FoodTransportation-FullReport.pdf.

Hou, Sophia. "Kids Care About: Sea Turtles," *Time for Kids*, July 23, 2021. https://www.timeforkids.com/g2/kids-care-about-sea-turtles-2/.

Jordan, Rob. "Stanford Researchers Find Mental Health Prescription: Nature," *Stanford News*, 30 June 2015. https://news.stanford.edu/2015/06/30/hiking-mental-health-063015/.

Louv, Richard. "The Nature Prescription," OARS. https://www.oars.com/blog/richard-louv-nature-prescription/.

National Geographic Society. "Watershed," National Geographic Resource Library. https://education.nationalgeographic.org/resource/watershed. Accessed Nov. 22, 2021.

Nature Conservancy. "Peregrine Falcon: Nature's Fastest Flying Machine," Sep. 9, 2018. https://www.nature.org/en-us/about-us/where-we-work/united-states/indiana/stories-in-indiana/peregrine-falcons/.

Nunez, Christina. "Carbon Dioxide Levels Are at a Record High," *National Geographic,* 13 May 2019. https://www.nationalgeographic.com/environment/article/greenhouse-gases.

Rios, Beatriz. "Trees for Goals: The Teenager Playing to End Deforestation," Euractiv, Sep. 30, 2019. https://www.euractiv.com/section/health-consumers/news/trees-for-goals-the-teenager-playing-to-end-deforestation/.

US Department of Energy. "Fossil," 2021. https://www.energy.gov/science-innovation/energy-sources/fossil.

US Environmental Protection Agency. "Air," 2021. https://www.epa.gov/environmental-topics/air-topics.

US Fish and Wildlife Service. Red Wolf Recovery Program. https://www.fws.gov/project/red-wolf-recovery-program. Accessed Feb. 11, 2022.

A Note to Grown-Ups

Rachel Carson, world-renowned ecologist and mother of the modern environmental movement, affirms, "If a child is to keep alive his inborn sense of wonder, he needs the companionship of at least one adult who can share it, rediscovering with him the joy, excitement, and mystery of the world we live in." Carson's statements to Congress in the 1960s prompted a sea change in ecology, protecting from toxic poisoning vast swaths of plant and animal life, including human. Throughout her writing, she championed the need for children to embrace the environment on an experiential level as well as to protect and revere it. Carson's own crusade began when she was a young girl, as her mother passed this torch of wonder to her.

This book is a catalyst for such wonder, teaching children how to appreciate the beauty of the earth, marvel at its scale, respond to its call for help, see self and nature with perspective, and identify as people who advocate for the natural world. The pages of this book also create a reparative space for children, providing solace from climate-change anguish and offering an invitation to revel in the natural world while defending it.

As the American Pediatric Association asserts, "Failure to take prompt, substantive action against climate change is an act of injustice to all children." Fortunately, climate solutions are widely known now; they are easily taught and integrated into daily life. The steps to make changes to our priorities, behaviors, laws, and practices have been mapped out and proven, ready for all to take. Studies show those who work to combat climate crisis experience the added benefit of improved psychological health as they advocate for a cleaner world, knowing they reduce suffering and protect the delicate web of life.

When children see the relevance of their earth-friendly acts they experience less anxiety and stress. And, increasingly, adults find "a little child will lead them." Young people across the globe aren't waiting on those in power to act, crusaders such as Greta Thunberg, Mari Copeny, Felix Finkbeiner, and countless others. Their passion for the earth promoted them to a place of self-empowerment. If their stories are unknown, look them up, be inspired, and join the fight. The results of their efforts will outlive us all.

As Jane Goodall writes, "You cannot get through a single day without having an impact on the world around you. What you do makes a difference, and you have to decide what kind of difference you want to make." *Climate Hero Handbook* is a child's guide for making decisions that can be seen, felt, heard, inhaled, ingested, and embraced as healthy, healing, and protective of the earth. The decision to defend, protect, and restore the planet is altruism at its most basic. This is a noble cause to pass on to children. Connecting to the earth is their natural right, and they have shown they are ready, able, and willing to preserve their planet with the support of the adults around them.

oak leaves

walnut

willow catkins

Jennifer Manley Rogers spent her childhood climbing trees, rambling across fields, and collecting shells in the Carolinas. Her first in-house staff editorial position was at a university press as a college student. In addition to teaching and mentoring children in several Latin American schools and churches, Jennifer has helped over 500 authors edit their books. She now owns and operates Catchphrase Publishing Services. https://www.catchphrasepublishingservices.com/.

Jessica Gamaché is an advocate for Creation Care and environmental awareness. She began her career as an environmental educator at a Lutheran church camp. Now serving as the Executive Director of a nonprofit, Jessica brings resources and education to United Methodist camping leaders across the country. She believes that being immersed in the outdoors through a camp experience brings all people closer to God and one another.

Louise OFarrell grew up in London and Dublin and studied graphic design. She continued her studies in the United States through a Rotary International program and made friends from all around the world. Now based in Florida, Louise designs books about ecology and many other subjects. She has worked locally to improve recycling and waste reduction in schools.

Sophie Anne Elliott is an artist who lives with animals and grows vegetables on the western coast of the United States. From a young age her love of drawing mythical creatures grew into a whimsical naturalist style. This is Sophie's first published book of illustrations. https://sophieanneelliott.weebly.com/.

CPSIA information can be obtained
at www.ICGtesting.com
Printed in the USA
BVHW020149070922
646402BV00001B/3